Relationship
a long poem

Relationship
a long poem

Jayanta Mahapatra

Introduction by **Jaydeep Sarangi**

BLACK EAGLE BOOKS
Dublin, USA | Bhubaneswar, India

Black Eagle Books
USA address:
7464 Wisdom Lane
Dublin, OH 43016

India address:
E/312, Trident Galaxy, Kalinga Nagar,
Bhubaneswar-751003, Odisha, India

E-mail: info@blackeaglebooks.org
Website: www.blackeaglebooks.org

First International Edition Published by
Black Eagle Books, 2023

RELATIONSHIP
by **Jayanta Mahapatra**

Copyright © Jayanta Mahapatra

All rights reserved. No part of this publication may be reproduced, stored in a retrieval system, or transmitted, in any form or by any means, electronic, mechanical, photocopying, recording or otherwise without the prior permission of the publisher.

Cover & Interior Design: Ezy's Publication

ISBN- 978-1-64560-449-5 (Paperback)
Library of Congress Control Number: 2023946428

Printed in the United States of America

INTRODUCTION

Jaydeep Sarangi

Sahitya Akademi award winning book, *Relationship* is a trend setter that takes us back to the time of making of the canon in Indian English poetry-- how Indian English poetry evolved in and around Jayanta Mahapatra who arrived in the poetry scene in 1971 with the title, *Close the Sky Ten by Ten*. In the 1970s his poems were published in major poetry journals in the world and he earned accolades from different shores. During the 1970s Jayanta was invited to read poems from many important places including, University of Iowa, Iowa City, 1976, University of Tennessee, Chattanooga, 1976, University of the South, Sewanee, 1976, East West Center, Honolulu, Hawaii, 1976, P.E.N. Centre, Sydney, 1978 and Australian National University, Canberra, 1978. These made valuable grounds for making him a significant poetic voice in the decades to come. *A Rain of Rites* appeared from the University of Georgia Press, USA in 1976. Vernon Young praised the work in *The*

Hudson Review, and later Emily Grosholz reviewed both *Relationship* and *The False Start* in the same New York journal. *Poetry* (Chicago) published a review of his books and it was done by the poet Dick Allen. His publications were noticed by Paul Engle, poet and Director of the International Writing Program in Iowa, and he invited Jayanta to be a participating poet from India for 1976. It was a significant phase for Jayanta, 1975—1976, because it coincided with the publication of his collection of poems, *A Rain of Rites*, from the University of Georgia Press, Athens, USA. During these days his manuscript was chosen from among the many poetry manuscripts submitted to the University by the final reader and editor, George Core, who is ,and has been the Editor of the literary quarterly, The *Sewanee Review*. In 1976 he was in Iowa city, with twenty other writers from different countries.

With Jayanta Mahapatra a new confidant idiom for Indian English Poetry was born. Cuttack became a prominent place in the English poetry map in India. His *Chandrabhaga* became an important cultural map maker. Things followed the man at Tinknia Bagicha who democratized English poetry in India. Relationship, an epic-like poem, is set in Orissa--a land of 'forbidden myth'. The heroic past of the land and rivers are recalled again and again in the poem.

Relationship: A Long Poem is Jayanta Mahapatra's relationships and roles at different social levels and personal conditions. His 'timorous' voice became a major voice of the nation within a decade or so;

"Dust and the sun tear open our timorous voices.
What is it I want to hear
when I look into the eyes of the hunter
as an iron mist takes possession of me again(.)"

An intelligent soul maker, Jayanta Mahapatra is a poet of the relic of the colonial past, silent watcher on the fringes of life. He is a champion poet with propensity for negative dialectic;

"So I shall seek the sleep-habit
of the golden deer, tempter of the tastes,
in order that I might see outlined
against the vast forest of the heart
the miracle of living, so that others may pity me(.)"

For Jayanta Mahapatra, he writes for Odisha, to the land in which his roots lie and lies his past and in which lies his 'beginning and end'. *Relationship* is deeply rooted to his land, milieu, myth, the people and relationships. It is difficult to leave the place, once it is fixed to his name, links and roles. The poet explores how everything is, lives and breathes or just ceases to be. Every special intimacy is a smile and forgetting in time:

"Today I watch through the window
the grave that is my mother's,
watch the old impulses in red and yellow
chalked across the white terraces of childhood,
in the shores of distant refrains(.)"

Relationship depicts the relationship between the poetic self to his personal past in connection with a rich cultural memory of the land. Standing on the banks of poems Jayanta is a river of poems by himself. He assumes the role of Mahanadi of poems and inspirations for many budding poets from different backgrounds. Jayanta became very popular for his crow poems. His ' crow noises' is a postcolonial substitution for any white bird of the West. The sensuous poet says, " It's here I live, in the unseeing heart."

Waiting makes a man introspective. Engrossed in deep thoughts, the poet looks before and after and penetrates the hard facts of reality by forgetting the present. Jayanta describes a vivid state of waiting. Jayanta, the poet, thinks that at times, the human mind is damp with cold and rain. At times, the poet takes notice of the seeds of our lives to be sown away into earth's ancient subsoil and dispensable prides of human journeys. Some things keep happening always in the poet's mind. Jayanta lives through the pain and waits for rain to restore ease. In *Relationship* life unfolds its roots and dreams,

> "(o)nly that the stones were my very own,
> waiting as mother or goddess or witch,
> as my birth feeds on them
> as though on the empty dugs of sorcerous thought."

Poet Jayanta universalizes the state of waiting. To spin a thought's wing waiting is a kind of suspended animation. It is a stock currency of life. We wait for the

rains before we can plough
"But time has no mouth,
and the black labyrinth
of casuarinas along the edges of the sea
closes the sky's eternal vault(.)"

Jayanta Mahapatra's material descriptions of the indigenously Indian society and landscape are accompanied by his historical vision becoming a rare gift. For him, landscapes result in memory. Orissa is a great land of myth and legends. Jayanta is a custodian of his rich traditions;

"We are delivered by the myth
which exhorts our sleep and our losses,
that wakes us like toys springing out of a box(.)"

Door is Jayanta's stock image. A door of paper is a space where everyone is waiting ; each for the others:

"So many times I have stumbled out of my door,
proud of that time I had held hidden in my hand,
to see the sage of troubled mien
sitting under the peepul tree, all alone (.)"

Trained as a physicist, Jayanta Mahapatra writes poetry that is intensely personal, and precise. He reminds us greatly of the Chilean poet-diplomat Pablo Neruda and his fascinations for the past relics. The present, according to Mahapatra, contains an enfeebled shadow of the glorious past:

"Now I stand among these ruins,
waiting for the cry of a night-bird
from the river's far side
to drift through my weariness(.)"

Jayanta writes for a better society-- equal opportunity and equity for all. His views are thoroughly anthropocentric.

Like many noted poets in different Indian vernaculars the theme of death and departure are recurring themes in Jayanta's *Relationship* where the poems(as parts of a long poem) meditate upon nature, the monsoon rains, the rainy seasons, the temples or street happenings, the crispness of the air and the clarity these poems bring, refresh the poet's subtle mind:

"In your dance is my elusive birth, my sleep
that swallows the green hills of the land
and the crows that quicken the sunlight in the veins,
and the stone that watches my sadness fly in and out
of my deaths, a spiritless soul of memory(.)"

Relationship is redolent with love, life, longing and hope, where leaf by leaf the magician knocks at the multiple doors of hearts and heads.

Principal and professor of English, New Alipore College, Kolkata and a scholar / follower of Jayanta Mahapatra. Website: https://jaydeepsarangi.in/
Place: Jhargram/Kolkata   September 2023

One

Once again one must sit back and bury the face
in this earth of the forbidding myth,
the phallus of the enormous stone,
when the lengthened shadow of a restless vulture
caresses the strong and silent deodars in the valley,
and when the time of the butterfly
moves inside the fierce body of the forest bear,
and feel the tensed muscle of rock
yield to the virtuous water of the hidden springs
of the Mahanadi,
the mystery of secret rights that make up destiny;
and to clasp the slow slopes of stone again
that ascend to the realm of the dead,
slopes that stroke the mind
with their quiet faces of sorrow,
like that of old men curling for warmth
in the winter sun,
and of young ochre-clad prophets
laden with silent fulfilment of tomorrow.

We have come as dreams disguised that pinned us down,
artisans of stone,
messengers of the spirit,

twelve hundred artless brown flowers in passion
to the night in humble brotherhood,
aerial roots of a centuries-old banyan tree;
not taking lives seriously
for our lives are only of the seeds of dreams,
forgetting the cruelties
of ruthless emperors who carved peaceful edicts
on blood-red rock,
forgetting our groans and cries,
the smells of gunsmoke and smoldering flesh,
forgetting the tactics and the strategy
that led to the founding of the infinite distance
inside our watery skulls.

Time
and the boat,
and the initiation into the mystery of peace;
the sailing ships of those maritime ancestors
who have vanished in the black Bay without a trace,
that only live in the sound of the waves
flinging themselves on to the dark fringes
of this land from Chilika to Chandipur.
But time has no mouth,
and the black labyrinth
of casuarinas along the edges of the sea
closes the sky's eternal vault,
tall and brutal,
trapping the evening's first stars of haunting order
and the solitary traveller
who can sense the brilliant colors of the past
in the ocean's strange and bitter deeps,
that subterranean river in the rock
which admits him with dignity

into some fresh wonder of its flowing.
Now caught in the in the currents of time
I watch the blue of the sky
seep out slowly,
hear the voices of old waves drift into silence;
and yet my existence lies in the stones
which carry my footsteps from one day into another,
down to the infinite distances, the dense jungles
where tigers' eyes are glowing red.
like virulent boils of pox on dead women and children,
and where the grotesque dawn of wilderness wood
becomes a conceiver of life, nothing else,
as I continue walking back and forth
not knowing whether the earth
would let me find finally its mouth;

only that the stones were my very own,
waiting as mother or goddess or witch,
as my birth feeds on them
as though on the empty dugs of sorcerous thought.

Two

Today I watch through the window
the grave that is my mother's,
watch the old impulses in red and yellow
chalked across the white terraces of childhood,
in the shores of distant refrains,
as a member of some magician's audience
watches a white rabbit
flash out of the excited applause
and vanish in the air,
or as a fraudulent reflection
recoils from a warm summer afternoon,
just as a thin veil of light drops
the distant mountains through the open door
of my flesh,
and the unidentifiable dead shadows
strip the skin off my face,
and from the body of the last green spring
memory takes a road vague with the distance
of loneliness and hurt,
away from the terrible glance of sky and its forest
where cranes bound into the surrounding silence
and the clouds shift with the tears
of wounded pools of our living.

Orion crawls like a spider in the sky
while the swords of forgotten kings

rust slowly in the museums of our guilt,
while the carved rock loses its light,
and the man with many memories
doesn't know what to do with them,
with the river flowing sluggishly through his dark,
for the boats he let loose upon the water
merely bob up and down, going nowhere;
as the grass of history
merely glistens for a moment with night dew, merely that
and my memories are just voices of another world,
pretending from the throat
where the distant music of stars cuts blood,
and the suffering of the world returns
like winter's persistent asthma
year after year.

Now like my quickly-aging father
my mind fumbles at the frail substance of ash,
and my memories are rats scampering in the dark
gnawing at rotting paper,
twisted metal and foul flesh,
and my blood becomes to share his curse;

as I forget easily
my old village's pelt, glistening with rain,
and the stillness of my gentle daughter's skin,
forget the desire
oozing out of the hewn stones of Konarka,
and the voices of frogs
bending the white-wet moonlight into embraces,
through the strange fires that carried him down
from the tranquil hills in the rain.

Three

Here is the tapestry of the year's first rain;
like an army, uniformed in gray,
but penitents, down on their knees.
What can ever wash the air of its gashed voices?
It is hard to tell now
what opened the anxious skies,
how the age-old proud stones
lost their strength and fell,
and how the waters of the Daya
stank with the bodies of my ancestors;
my eyes close now
because of the fear that moves my skin:
the invaders walk along the only road they know
that leads to their bloody victories.

Ah Father!
You recognize the sounds
of your children's laughter before it comes,
and the whispers of gods
before they crumple under your children's feet.

These nights of the growing moon
fill us with the feeling of good;
that is exactly what you wished for us,
didn't you, Father?
So our courage would be swept away

by the fierce winds of summer dust?
So we would go on
reading the epics in the lamplight,
sucking our mother's dry and drooping breasts,
watch the thin moon blend into that darkness
where gigolos and pimps and bums
jabber excitedly in a language of monstrous flowers.

I remember only last week I counted up my friends,
and I felt as though I were in painful exile:
friendship is like a pool of water
where shadows move about and dance,
and winds of doubt cloud some of the drifting faces,
the sun of envy sucks the others away.

Dust and the sun tear open our timorous voices.
What is it I want to hear
when I look into the eyes of the hunter
as an iron mist takes possession of me again,
as the words of mine that yearn for rain
catch only the jagged lightning of this new cult
and its messianic gain?

Out of the darkness, the ash:
I won't touch it, my fingers let the grains slip by,
my hands are weak for the violent life,
the window looking out onto my mother's grave
defends my dream,
one which I have never understood through the years,
as though it were a sky full of fallen birds,
as from its depths
a cloud drops its rain
onto the great silence over the stone of fire.

Now you don't even want me to write my poem,
of those words which spit blood and vomit and speak of malice,
but only those which shut out the wind
and lay them in the dark crevices of stone
for births to merge into darker births
that look for the age-old grass of my death
beyond its contemplation and its withering.

Four

So the sleep you wear yourself to
through the smoldering burning-ground
of your granite eyes
or through the birds alighting tamely
on the warm indigo waters of the tropics:
colorless and dreamless, a light without leaves,
will not reveal the truth of that secret miracle
of the darkness that hangs over the screams
of the hyenas or the snarls of the bears,
when, afraid of the silence that lurks inside
the dawn of your startled smile,
the thousand windows of my sorrowful heart
look upon your untempered mile
that wanders through the eternal half-light of rain.

Is this
simply a craving to let myself go,
to bury a drug-drop of today's bitterness
in the pit of my heart?
My fear receives no one;
like a flame which sings on altars of the dead,
isn't it strong enough
to shed the blood from the veins?

Burden of your peace, Father
Theme-song of my life that bums my tongue

Voices of children always wronged
And now, you, my ancient love of a hundred names,
of rains and endless skies and morning mists,
of wind-beaten evenings of owl-calls and rice-harvests
in December,
my love of gold nose-rings and laughing earrings,
of towering ruins of stone panting in the dark,
of loyal lions guarding the diamond navels of shrines,
of amber breasts and secret armpits,
of cries and the soft steel of thighs,
and of the old emptiness of my own destiny;

I know I can never come alive
if I refuse to consecrate at the altar of my origins
where the hollow horn blows every morning
and its suburban sound picks its way
through the tangled moonlight of your lazy sleep.

Here now is this aging, my chance and sentence,
calmly circling hawk-like overhead for prey,
as the earth glistens with old mountains
and moaning rivers that satisfy
the solitudes lingering in the open talk of men.

But lying upon my loneliness
this brassy October afternoon,
the secret coves on the naked beach
charred by old fires and littered with
picnic-paper and empty bottles,
I want to finish my prayer that began
like a thin rustling in a mango tree,
a prayer to draw my body out of a thousand years
and reflect the earth's lost amplitudes,

the bridal footprints of fantastic peacocks dancing
in the rain
and the warm palms of gathering dusk
where crimson heart-lines float longingly
in the unknown sunlight of the earth,
like soft cirrus crossing space above,
and my dark heart twists
with a feather of your unheard moan,
weary with an echo
of your goodbye of tasteless ash.

Five

So I shall seek the sleep-habit
of the golden deer, tempter of the tastes,
in order that I might see outlined
against the vast forest of the heart
the miracle of living, so that others may pity me,
so that my dream would not end:
the fabulous marriage procession of power, like Siva's,
and the different dimensions of lies and betrayals
in order to survive,
the strange country
in which you weave your flaming play.

This sleep was needed,
to go on pretending that blood throbs
in the pallor of dreams, to find
the enchanted regions of boyhood and dignity
where the burnt granite of the fallen Konarka
binds the sun to a rhythm of desire,
and the supple figures multiply
their mute echoes of another fire on stone.

What other answers can one think of
on a late autumn night,
when centuries drift quietly in the air,
rising like a mist from the steaming rivers
toward this visionary part of one?

Thus the naked wall,
groping through wind and rain,
that speaks back without sound or voice
and yet anoints our eyes with blood,
to wreck frantic vengeance
with its earth of acid ground;
a sleep of swamp grass and mangroves,
like a humid fever,
which protects the shores of life from savage storms.

What sea leads your blazing rivers
headlong into it? Were you worked up
by the gold quarries in that twilight place
where the phantom darkness
glowed red like blood? Were you guided
by the premature deaths of those frightened virgins
who fought the light of the stars
in their underground caves only to fall
at the darts of fretting virtue?
This sleep is a song
that is heard from all sides continually,
a coarse cage that can hold a larger life,
a time that stretches the scarlet in the mind
and graces the heart's skies with clear wind,
the hiding-place without beginning or end,
and the largest circle that transcends
the angles of man's consciousness,
a blind eye that creates the special vision
of our poignant significance.

Six

And how shall room be made for sleep,
how shall the wind be made to carry
the lioness's roar, the endless ritual
of the black kites on the faraway hill
silenced in the whiteness of the clouds?

Voices go in and out of the city gates;
the moment the storm blows, I know I will scramble
to hide the thunder in the thick jackfruit groves
on the other side of the wall,
blackening the seeds of the fruit,
and reddening the soft gums of the unassailable flesh.

I look through the swollen grass of noon
and in the heart of great gray clouds and cutting rains
the autumns of a thousand years
spread out like leaves, filthy and veined with blood,
over the smooth dark stone of our lives:
what can save us now
but the miracle we have been waiting for?

The clock,
stabbing in a cobra's tongue across the air,
an unknown bird
brushing past with a flap of wings

like the unseen wind scalloping the silence
out there in the bleak cremation ground;
no, there is room enough for cries and whispers,
for a nameless sigh, for the sharp blade of love,
for another kindredship of spirit
to spread over my face the flaring magnesium
of a smile,
for a new body to reveal
the green-leaved carpet of pleasure,
somewhere, elsewhere,
wearing the dreams away of the forgotten Ganga kings,
digging at the ruins of their own private sorrow.

Seven

How long does it take one to know
that it is he who is standing there,
alone by himself in the witness-box
of shackled pink muscle?

Once again
the heavy round night rolls on my pillow,
the weight of shadows of sick relics lies upon the bed,
time to realize that martyrdom is not for those
left alone in that no-man's land
where venison tastes like cottonwool,
and where the seated Buddha of my urge and will and pride
would topple from the poisonous bite and acid
of the subtle bird of night,
but to find again the five shadows
which would help avenge the cooled motionless blood,
the elephant of the six blind men,
the crude murders
and the haughty seasons over man's eyes,
the rules of our song
that can only move back and forth
like a galvanometer needle
between the zero and the hundred of gloom.

Therefore into the pit of feverish sinews

and spring seashells let me fall,
for only by conquering them
can one conquer the rest of the world,
and the empty shore then
thunder with the red lightning of the hermit crabs,
and the sense of empty sadness
turn into the mangled skeleton
of a sleep.

And let the wild harmoniums play on,
the wooden soldiers marching, not knowing where,
in my thick insomnia,
to the beat of drums
heralding the periodic invasions of the enemy
into the vanquished city
and I remember your trembling
through the deserted ashes of my heart
that will already have been sold,
and the dark worn steps are marked
by the green rain of centuries,
shadows of my blood waving their pretentious hands.

Eight

It is my own life
that has cornered me beneath the stones
of this temple in ruins, in a blaze of sun.
Sun-lions, standing against the steps,
whose return to life are you waiting for?
Whose roar to pulse through the veins
of this first night of sleep?

Far into these granite peaks of dream
where the air is moist and soft in the smell of the sea,
where the dying child lays his father on the sands'
blind solitude,
where there swills about us
the spacious body of woman, the fruit and the flower,
the gentle leaf, the folded belly
and the sweeping fire,
like the warm waters around fish,
like the velvet down about the floating breath
of fledglings.

So through this door, through
the gleaming skin of the three kingdoms,
the mineral, vegetable and animal,
to experience the fever of love
and the deeper undulation of the earth.

Would meaning remain
in merely that a thing exists, on a single plane,
in the helpless sips of loneliness we have made,
marooned on the stone, on the dark chariot of the sun
whose fevered granite wheels claw desperately
at the strangled earth in our lives?

These things, hewn out of the darkness
and of the light, of our ominous destinations,
of the real and the imagined:
the bronzed gazes of mermaids
against the infinite blue of the sea,
the night of wild elephants pounding down
in the undying sun,
and the horned and the hooved,
the gandharvas and the demons,
aren't these mere imitations we have made
not having had enough of the sun's flight
across the purple hills of our guilt,
and the haunting dawn whose convex arcs of light
correspond to the dark abyss
of an absent dimension of the blood?

This is the real body: raging pachyderm
with the crazy testicles, red and wild,
the lusting god of the blackest Siva night:
thus it is that it can hardly contain ourselves.
For it is no use trying to keep it away,
the quinine of this silence, the cloud of my sweat:
would your unborn rain show me
the colors and contours
of the distant valleys of birth?

For now I touch your secret order,
embarrassed yoni;
before me lie the sulking years of dreams,
the stricken purposes of the muscles,
the violent splashes of sunsets
in the fibres of the being.

How would I pull you out
of the centuries of fallen stone?
How would I hold the linga in the eye
until the world is made all over again?

Nine

This must be the myth of every happiness,
the high wind that flings the flowers into disarray,
the adamant bones which keep rolling in the dust
of the dark butterflies,
the cry of the wounded sun silenced among
the ruins of Konarka.
I thought: those who survive the myth
have slipped past their lives and cannot define
their reason,
the trees are getting sparse, the clouds dwindle
into colder air,
the ancestral fires are no more snares,
purposes that resembled the webs of the sun
are lost in the silences of corners of dim rooms
where only ideas, like brooms,
wait oddly on their unstable heads.

Once it was a season, it was a bride
I dragged in its joyous flower-pot into the middle
of my life:
my dead grandfather floated in that sea of buried things,
wings ablaze with a silver fire,
as if his body of stone were a pyre
burning on in that razed city of the ambitious walls.

Those who've been my friends throughout the years
have known only how to keep walking toward themselves,
along the upraised road, unsullied by guilt and belief:
the rapture of ownership on their voluble faces,
their satisfaction stained green
by the green of the mango trees of the delta,
the green of banana and the green wind in the tamarinds,
and strangely cold by their own mistrust
of the inextinguishable ash.

I tried to speak of the myth of sleep and action,
in the hope of soothing myself and those others,
rummaging through the secret blood
of the wind in the pines
and awaiting the deepening nature of all things;
a perfection I'd prove to myself,
the honesty that holds the throat of man
against the light and looks down at my hands
and scales the anguish passing from man to man
to reveal the coarse need
that still can make one love a neighbour;
and at the savage blooming of some common stone
that calls to me from its mystery and its dream,
and which resembles the unexplained feeling
of a mother
when she gives her breast
to her dry neighbour's bawling child.

And I heard someone speak of it there below:
where the bamboos sag like sad-eyed widows in worship
into the stagnant village pools,
in which naked children sleep for ever
among the green coils of the water-lily,

and where a dark-eyed woman climbs the endless stairs
of her abandoned house, the great earth
cowering before her, turning back
the triumph of death with the power
of her faithful silence, outside the bonds of time,
and where the mysterious shadows lurk under the leaves,
dispersing the past over the bends of the Mahanadi.

But what was this myth? It was like a leaf
whose trembling held my hand;
the colossal temple had crumbled in the unknown past,
onto the sandy bank of a vanished river
which once had dominated the heart of the wind.

What was the myth, a journey in which one feared
one could lose oneself at any moment? Or was it
merely a time which lay in the dust and stone
of the languid water, which moved sadly
about the absent jasmines only to be heaped
against those unreachable shores?

It is no use now if I try to wear
my grandfather's smile, disappearing for an instant
in the midst of this myth; there are shadows
over my body, from the burning sun,
there are structures which flank the river,
lacquered in red and gold,
sundays with savage afternoons
and shrivelled steps dangling from the shrines,
mirrors whose images throw
involuted rainbows into faces,
there are prostitutes with white hair
who are excited simply by having stared

at their inaccessible sons,
and friends whose eyes are black and bitter with malice
like envelopes with poisonous glue on their flaps
because they are positioned by an ignorance
in my heart,
and newspapers that bend our minds
with gleaming and immaculate words,
and daggers that are anxious to return
to the naked flesh,
and shameless fevers
whose viruses tear the skin like paper.

Ten

So many times I have stumbled out of my door,
proud of that time I had held hidden in my hand,
to see the sage of troubled mien
sitting under the peepul tree, all alone,
unspoken repose against the body oozing of love;
and, going past, in the act as though
of repeating a mistake, walking slowly toward them
in the swathe of indifference snaking out of their eyes
to make me accept the silence of which I was in fear.

For it seemed to be a time
when waters flow past without their purposes,
when replicas of temples lie scattered everywhere
and thousands of fake huge eyes open wide in wood
inside them,
and bees become the lost witnesses
of an unknown honey before the storm.

And if it was the time, I thought,
to be conquered by a sleep that had come to rest
on the unmoving dreams of our past,
it would only help to free the darkness
that lingered on the mossed walls of my life,
and on the twisted bones
that plunged through my volcanic flesh.

For there, ahead in the growing distance
where the myth appeared to cut the instant
in light and shade,
a giant tree speechless above the sacred hill,
scores of women waited, their heads
covered with devotion,
like the leaves, shaking as though possessed
with spirits malign;
and the town of Cuttack where I was born,
its lanes scarred by ruts from whose clay
the goddesses take their sacred shapes
in autumn every year,
and looking out into the endless Bay;
mysterious inheritance
in which roots stick out here and there from the dung,
of broken empires and of vanquished dynasties,
and of ahimsa's whimpers;
for before I go to sleep
or go into the unknown in me:
this house of blind windows built inside,
doesn't the fear it provides accelerate
our happiness?

We are delivered by the myth
which exhorts our sleep and our losses,
that wakes us like toys springing out of a box,
opening out like humiliating episodes
or dutiful monuments that celebrate
the victories of that darkness over us.

Perhaps it came out of a ruined birthplace,
from the last barren heath we could not cross,
to set feet on top of the massive stone;

that was to be the first hiding-place
and whose ruins would remain forever
to defy the progress of our race,
as we felt the black slime of lotus-root
move slowly through our bone,
copying the reeds in the river as they bend
in the current,
to give way to the river-silence
of aging timber lining the morose banks.

Now I stand among these ruins,
waiting for the cry of a night-bird
from the river's far side
to drift through my weariness,
listening to the voices of my friends
who have become the friends of others,
writing poems, abject and anxious,
in rooms which reek of old folk,
of their sloth and arthritis and neglect,
like stale cupboards which are going black
with the smells of the rancid fat of the past.

Eleven

Yet what holds back my voice is only a mirror,
the sound of the answer from these pitted ruins,
through the hollow, unreal space of the stone
like the flesh hollowed out by the years in a woman,
fragrant of old sandalwood and the dawn light of fish
that opens a flight of steps behind,
down which the unfelt beat of the heart
becomes deaf to everything,
all else being taken up by a possession.
Then can the present be recognized, what one endures
and one will continue to endure, a kind of world
that comes up of all the love he has known,
so that man can see from the vast night around him
the beauty soar into the sky,
into the tangles of cloud and rain,
of that drowsy voice calling
from other people's lives.

For lofty as they are on their twentyfour blue spells,
my walk along the tremblings of the stone
seems loftier still; to the flashing tendril
from the fugitive root, the throat of stone
choked with the many truths of eternal sleepers,
gently over the precarious tiers
as I put my hand toward a dream the sun
has kept awake through the years.

And at last there
where the day sweeps its aggressive yellow curves
like a serpent-woman's tail,
is the space, defiant, waiting,
and the iron sea of years ago curling about the feet,
a phosphorescent glow, an essence divine,
small yet huge enough to fill
with the velvet storms of pink lotuses,
and with the desire of my hands
I draw the day unto myself, trembling with being,
the sky and the vine that will become
the exile for night to hold,
trembling with each new moment to a gold,
each woman's breath of moist grass
and her thresholds of milk
to a red meat of grace.

Twelve

Fear of my guilt, I bid you farewell.
When the waves come, following one another,
the silence and the noise,
the banished princess and the magnolia tree as well,
a song rises from the honeycomb latticework of stone
to grip these bones where
a gray water of blood stretches out to the future.
Is anything beyond me that I cannot catch up?
Tell me your names, dark daughters
Hold me to your spaces
In your dance is my elusive birth, my sleep
that swallows the green hills of the land
and the crows that quicken the sunlight in the veins,
and the stone that watches my sadness fly in and out
of my deaths, a spiritless soul of memory.

NOTES

Relationship is set in the state of Orissa.

Konarka: The superb 13th century stone temple on the sea, shaped to a monumental chariot and dedicated to the Sun God, is now in a state of ruin. The twenty-four carved wheels with their rich decorations, the seven horses, the magnificent panel of elephants at the base, the figures in the innumerable niches, show the moods and phases of human life compellingly. Its gods and goddesses, gandharvas and apsaras, the supple women with their entwining serpent bodies, the elaborate latticework- all these represent the Oriya craftsman's search for the beatific vision in the realm of art and aesthetics... Legend goes that the crowning slab of the temple could only be fitted into place by a 12-year old boy, the son of the chief architect of the work, after all attempts to do so by the 1200 artisans had failed in 12 long years. Later, the boy jumped to his death from the top of the finished temple to save his father's name and honour in a supreme act of sacrifice.

ruthless emperors: In 261 B.C. the emperor Asoka invaded Kalinga and massacred thousands of Oriyas at Dhauli, on the river Daya. Crestfallen when he saw the river turn red in the blood of the vanquished, he suffered from a change of heart and carved his famous rock edicts for posterity.

maritime ancestors: Kalinga was a maritime nation in the olden days. Enough evidence exists to show that there was regular trade between Kalinga and the islands of Indonesia, the Philippines, and other countries in the far east.

grotesque dawn of wilderness wood: The sacred deity of Jagannath at Puri is fashioned from the wood of a neem tree chosen from the dense Orissa jungles every twelve years.

Portrayed misshapen and limbless, with huge round eyes, Jagannath is the synthesis of all faiths and cultures, and is the revered symbol of worship of the Oriya people.

birds alighting on the waters of the tropics: Refers to the annual migration of large flocks of birds from as far north as Siberia to the warm waters of Lake Chilika , on Orissa's southern shores.

rice-harvests in December: Orissa, predominantly agricultural, has for its staple crop, rice; which is harvested toward end-December.

red lightning of the hermit crabs: The mud-flats and beaches at Chandipur (and Paradeep) swarm with red crabs, presenting a brilliant, unforgettable sight.

from whose clay the goddesses take their sacred shapes: Every autumn clay images of gods and goddesses are made and worshipped in long-drawn-out festivities.

banished princess and the magnolia tree: From an old Oriya folktale, in which a princess was turned into a flowering tree by an evil charm.

Black Eagle Books

www.blackeaglebooks.org
info@blackeaglebooks.org

Black Eagle Books, an independent publisher, was founded as a nonprofit organization in April, 2019. It is our mission to connect and engage the Indian diaspora and the world at large with the best of works of world literature published on a collaborative platform, with special emphasis on foregrounding Contemporary Classics and New Writing.

www.ingramcontent.com/pod-product-compliance
Lightning Source LLC
Chambersburg PA
CBHW060345080526
44583CB00014B/1071